The Story of Flight

MILITARY AIRCRAFT of WWI

Crabtree Publishing Company
www.crabtreebooks.com

PMB 16A, 350 Fifth Avenue
Suite 3308
New York, NY 10118

612 Welland Avenue
St. Catharines, Ontario
L2M 5V6

Published in 2003 by
Crabtree Publishing Company

Coordinating editor: Ellen Rodger
Project editors: Sean Charlebois, Carrie Gleason
Production coordinator: Rose Gowsell

Created and Produced by
David West 𝄞𝄞 Children's Books

Project Development, Design, and Concept
David West Children's Books:
Designer: Rob Shone
Editor: James Pickering
Illustrators: Gerry Haylock, Neil Reed,
Hemesh Alles & Mark Dolby (Allied Artists),
James Field & Ross Watton (SGA), Steve Weston
(Specs Art), Colin Howard (Advocate)
Picture Research: Carlotta Cooper

Photo Credits:
Abbreviations: t-top, m-middle, b-bottom, r-right,
l-left, c-center.

Front cover tm & pages 18tl, 12tl, (O.Stewart
Collection), 4-5t (PC 76/17/3), 6tl (P3653), 10t
(PC 76/23/8), 11tr (X001-2785/116), 13tr (PC
71/19/172), 14tl (FA00980) & bl (P295), 16bl
(X002-8006/001), 18bl (PC 72/16247), 22tl (PC
74/41/430) & bl (PC 75/1), 25tr (PO21792) & br,
26tl (X003-0205/002), 27tr (PC 71/31/2) - Royal
Air Force Museum. 5tr - Castrol. 6bl, 21bl - Rex
Features Ltd. 8tl, 29bl - Ole Steen Hansen. 16tl,
20tl - Hulton Archive.

06 05 04 03
10 9 8 7 6 5 4 3 2 1

Cataloging in Publication Data
Hansen, Ole Steen.
    Military aircraft of WWI / Ole Steen Hansen.
        p. cm. -- (The story of flight)
Includes index.
ISBN 0-7787-1201-X (RLB) -- ISBN 0-7787-1217-6 (PB)
    1. World War, 1914-1918--Aerial operations--Juvenile literature.
2. Airplanes, Military--History--20th century--Juvenile literature.
[1. World War, 1914-1918--Aerial operations. 2. Airplanes, Military.]
I.Title.
    D600.H35 2003
    940.4'42--dc21
                                    2002156482
                                    LC

The Story of Flight

MILITARY AIRCRAFT of WWI

Ole Steen Hansen

 Crabtree Publishing Company
www.crabtreebooks.com

CONTENTS

AIRSHIPS

German airships carried more than 35,000 people on 1,500 passenger flights before World War I. Germany relied heavily on a fleet of military airships from the beginning of the war. Instead of passengers, these aircraft carried bombs.

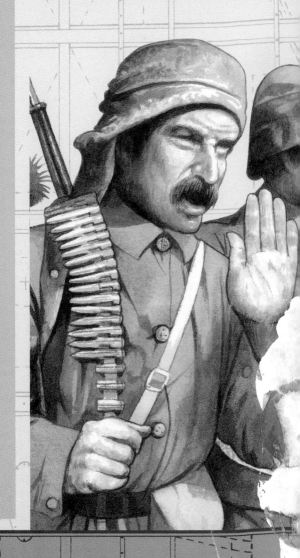

INTRODUCTION

World War I was fought between 1914 and 1918. Many pilots, as well as millions of soldiers on the ground, were involved in the war. The airplane was still a new invention, but it played an important part in the struggle. Special airplanes – fighters, heavy bombers, and ground attack aircraft – had to be designed. Pilots lined up to fly them into battle, despite heavy losses.

VICKERS VIMY

The Vickers Vimy bomber first flew in 1917, but it was not used in action during World War I. Vimys made some record breaking flights after the war.

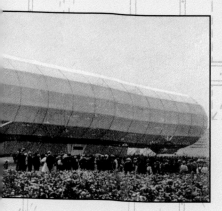

THE FIRST BOMBING RAID

In 1911, the first bombs were dropped from an aircraft. An Italian Blériot plane bombed Turkish positions in Libya, North Africa.

THE WAR BEGINS

AN AIRFIELD IN FRANCE
Front line air bases during World War I were just open fields. A British mechanic remembered a stormy night: "The whole squadron was turned out and we stayed there all night – five or six people to every aircraft hanging on to wings and tail plane – holding it down so it would not be lifted away."

B.E.2A
Length: 29 ft 3 in (9 m)
Wingspan: 34 ft 9 in (10.7 m)
Speed: 70 mph (112 km/h)
Country: Great Britain

At the beginning of World War I, most airplanes flew very slowly and could only stay in the air for a few hours. Germany had 250 airplanes for use on the front lines of war; France had 141, Britain had 83, Russia had about 50, and the United States (which was still not in the war) hardly had any.

Early in the war, these planes were used mainly for observing enemy troops from the air. The aircraft and their pilots were mostly unarmed.

The Battle Of Tannenberg
On the Eastern Front, the Russians had more cavalry troops on the ground than the Germans. In the battle of Tannenberg, German aviators, flying a Rumpler Taube, gained a clear picture of the Russian movements. This helped the Germans win the battle.

GREAT BRITAIN
BELGIUM
Bruxelles
Calais
Arras
Western Front
Verdun
Paris
FRANCE

BATTLE LINES
World War I soon changed from a war of motion to a trench war, in which the front lines moved very little. Millions of young men died fighting in the trenches on the Western Front.

Aircraft high in the sky were far better at observing enemy movements than troops on the ground. In September 1914, a French plane helped the **artillery** spot and stop advancing German troops outside Paris. At first, the artillery officer on the ground did not want to trust reports from a pilot. Shortly after, a British Royal Flying Corps (RFC) plane discovered a change in the direction of the advancing German army. This helped the French prepare for the battle on the Marne river, which saved the city of Paris from being captured.

MORANE-SAULNIER P
Length: 23 ft 6 in (7.2 m)
Wingspan: 36 ft 6 in (11.2 m)
Speed: 96 mph (155 km/h)
Country: France

RUMPLER TAUBE
Length: 32 ft 2 in (9.9 m)
Wingspan: 46 ft 10 in (14.4 m)
Speed: 72 mph (115 km/h)
Country: Germany

MARKINGS

Early military aircraft went to war without any kind of markings to identify their nationality. As a result, ground troops used to shoot at all aircraft, not knowing if they were friend or foe. The Germans soon started painting black crosses on their aircraft. Eventually, all warring nations introduced national markings on their airplanes.

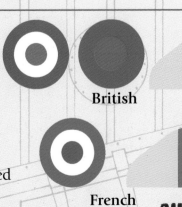

British

French

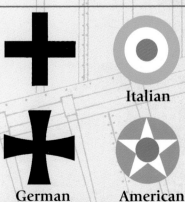

German

Italian

American

BOMBS

AVRO 504
The British used Avro 504s to bomb German Zeppelin hangars. This Avro 504 is still flying in Britain.

At the start of the war, bombing from balloons was forbidden by an international convention.

Bombing from airplanes began early in the war, because nobody could agree on an international ban on dropping bombs from airplanes.

French pilots bombed German Zeppelin airship hangars in August 1914. British aircraft did the same later that year. In the Far East, a German warship was sunk by Japanese aircraft.

L'ARMÉE ALLEMANDE se trouve aux Portes de PARIS il ne vous reste plus qu'à vous rendre

Leutnant VON HIDDESSEN

Propaganda
During the German air raid on Paris, small hand-held bombs were dropped from an airplane near a railway terminal. The pilot also dropped a message saying "The German Army is at the gates of Paris! There is nothing for you to do but surrender."

In December, the first German bombs fell on England, near Dover Castle. France had already put together specialized bombing and fighter squadrons. Airplanes were still used mainly for observing troops on the front line. The airplanes of 1914 could only lift very small loads. A few small bombs could not compare to a heavy artillery attack by ground troops, made possible with the help of an observation aircraft.

MUNITIONS

Bombs were very small at the beginning of the war. Small arrows, called fléchettes, were also dropped on the enemy early in the war. They were lethal if they hit anybody, but they were not all accurate. Bigger bombs were used later, but it took a heavy bomber to carry just one 1,650 lb (750 kg) bomb.

20 lb (9 kg) bombs

Hand thrown bomb and fléchette

1,650 lb (750 kg) bomb

PARIS IS BOMBED

A German Taube aircraft bombed Paris on August 30, 1914. This was the first time a capital city was bombed from an airplane.

THE FIRST ACE

Roland Garros was the first fighter pilot to be called an ace. After being taken prisoner by the Germans for three years, he escaped in 1918, and returned to flying. He was killed in combat a month before the war ended.

Lanoe G. Hawker

On July 25, 1915 Lanoe G. Hawker of the Royal Flying Corps was flying a Bristol Scout plane. His machine-gun was mounted at an angle, so that its bullets would not hit his propeller. The gun was difficult to aim, but Hawker shot down three German aircraft. He was awarded the **Victoria Cross** medal. In 1916, Hawker was killed in a dogfight with Manfred von Richthofen, the famous Red Baron.

MACHINE-GUNS

The daring Russian pilot P. N. Nesterov is said to have performed the first ever loop. In September 1914, he stopped an attack on his airfield by ramming a German plane and killing himself in the process. This was obviously not a good way to beat the enemy. Pilots had to find a way to down other planes and stay alive.

It was very difficult to hit other aircraft with revolvers, rifles, or hand grenades. Machine-guns were the answer, but the pilots needed to be able to shoot through the rotating propeller without damaging it. That way, a pilot could control his aircraft, and aim his gun at the same time. In 1915, French pilot Roland Garros and aircraft maker Raymond Saulnier attached small steel deflectors on to the propeller of a Morane-Saulnier N monoplane. Ten percent of the machine-gun bullets hit the deflectors and flew off in different directions, but the rest passed through. Garros was able to attack his victims head-on, and he soon shot down five German aircraft. He flew with his new invention for three weeks before a fracture in his fuel pipe forced him to land behind enemy lines, and he was captured.

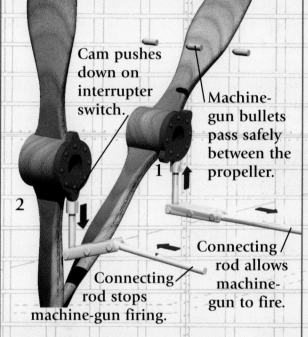

Cam pushes down on interrupter switch.

Machine-gun bullets pass safely between the propeller.

1

2

Connecting rod stops machine-gun firing.

Connecting rod allows machine-gun to fire.

INTERRUPTER SWITCHES
When the Germans discovered how Garros' machine-gun worked, they asked Anthony Fokker, a well-known engineer, to copy it. Instead, Fokker installed an interrupter switch, which let the machine-gun fire when the propeller blades were not in the way. A similar system had been invented before the war, but was ignored. Eventually, the interrupter switch became standard on most fighters.

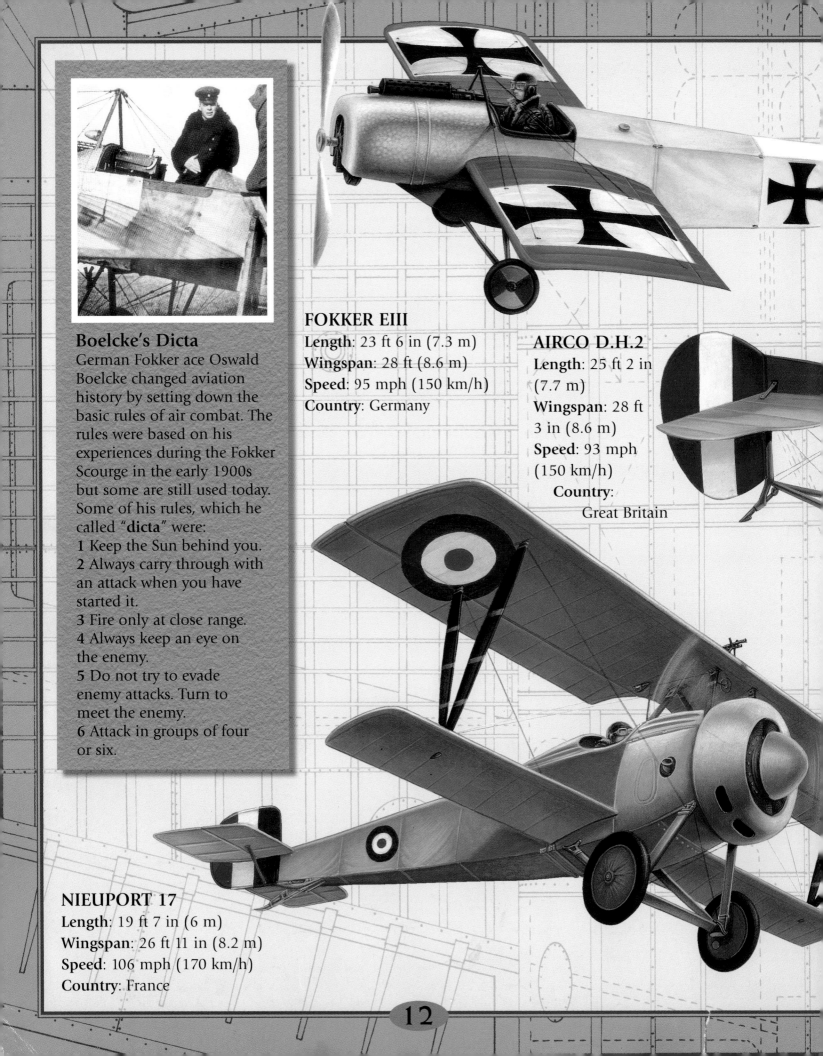

Boelcke's Dicta

German Fokker ace Oswald Boelcke changed aviation history by setting down the basic rules of air combat. The rules were based on his experiences during the Fokker Scourge in the early 1900s but some are still used today. Some of his rules, which he called "**dicta**" were:

1 Keep the Sun behind you.
2 Always carry through with an attack when you have started it.
3 Fire only at close range.
4 Always keep an eye on the enemy.
5 Do not try to evade enemy attacks. Turn to meet the enemy.
6 Attack in groups of four or six.

FOKKER EIII
Length: 23 ft 6 in (7.3 m)
Wingspan: 28 ft (8.6 m)
Speed: 95 mph (150 km/h)
Country: Germany

AIRCO D.H.2
Length: 25 ft 2 in (7.7 m)
Wingspan: 28 ft 3 in (8.6 m)
Speed: 93 mph (150 km/h)
Country: Great Britain

NIEUPORT 17
Length: 19 ft 7 in (6 m)
Wingspan: 26 ft 11 in (8.2 m)
Speed: 106 mph (170 km/h)
Country: France

THE FOKKER SCOURGE

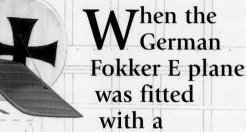

When the German Fokker E plane was fitted with a forward-firing machine-gun, it completely changed the air war over the Western Front. Many allied aircraft were shot down by the German fighter pilots.

IMMELMANN

Max Franz Immelmann was born in Dresden, Germany. With Fokker ace Oswald Boelcke, he became one of the most famous early German fighter pilots.

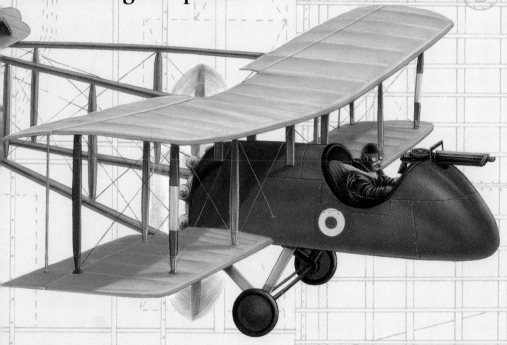

Observation became much more dangerous during what became known as the Fokker Scourge. The British tried to fight the Fokkers with the de Havilland DH 2 plane. Its engine was mounted behind the pilot, which made it simple to attach a forward-firing machine-gun. This fighter plane, and others such as the Nieuports, eventually stopped the Fokker EIIIs. The rear-mounted engine was also dangerous because during a crash landing the engine was often thrown forward into the pilot's back.

THE IMMELMANN TURN

With the forward-firing machine-gun of the Fokker EIII, it became possible to turn sharply and attack while flying. Immelmann invented the Immelmann turn for this. A version of it is still used in aerobatic competitions today.

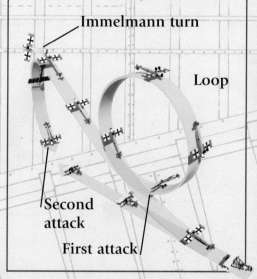

Immelmann turn

Loop

Second attack

First attack

AIR OFFENSIVE

Early in the war, German Zeppelins began bombing cities and troops. It soon became clear that these huge airships were easy to attack. When airships raided Britain, it was mainly under the cover of darkness.

COUNT ZEPPELIN
Count Ferdinand Adolf August Heinrich von Zeppelin was the inventor of the huge German airships that became known by his name all over the world.

This was the first ever continuous air attack by one country against another. The attacks shocked the British people, whose islands had always been protected by the Royal Navy. A pilot from the Royal Navy Air Service became the first person to down a Zeppelin by bombing it. Zeppelins were very difficult to spot at night. At first, it was also difficult to shoot them down, because the gas bags inside them leaked instead of burning, so they could be repaired in flight. When fire-bombs were used, the Zeppelins burned quickly. Eventually, the Germans began to lose more and more Zeppelins and stopped the night attacks on Britain.

FIRST ZEPPELIN BOMB OF THE WAR FELL

Bomb Damage
Compared with the air attacks of World War II, the Zeppelin raids were small and did little damage. A total of 557 people were killed and 1,358 were injured during the Zeppelin raids on Britain. The cost of the damage on the ground was less than the cost of the Zeppelins shot down.

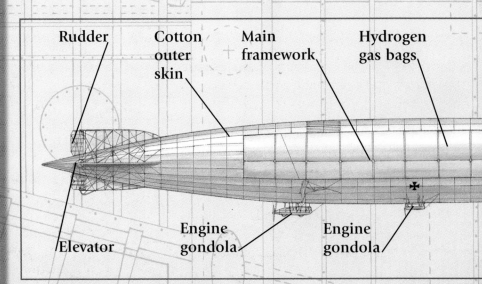

Rudder

Cotton outer skin

Main framework

Hydrogen gas bags

Engine gondola

Engine gondola

Elevator

DOWNING A ZEPPELIN

R. A. J. Warneford of the Royal Navy Air Service became the first pilot to down a Zeppelin in aerial combat. He hit it with bombs, and his own airplane was tossed wildly about by the exploding airship.

INSIDE A ZEPPELIN

A Zeppelin was built as a rigid frame, made of metal (a few were made of wood). It had hydrogen gas bags inside it to lift it. The Zeppelin was covered in fabric. **Gondolas** for the engines and crew hung below. A Zeppelin could lift a far heavier load than any airplane during World War I. Zeppelins could also travel further than airplanes.

Bridge

15

AIR WAR OVER THE SEA

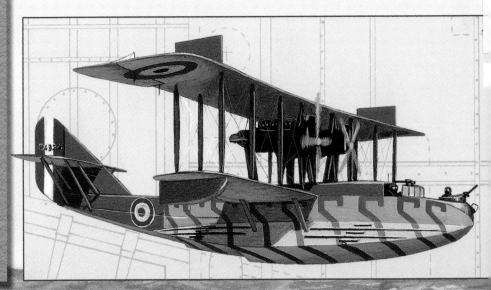

U-BOAT MENACE
In World War I, Germany tried to use submarines called U-boats to cut off supplies to Britain. U-boats sank many ships. Airplanes were used to observe U-boats from the air.

Over the sea, airplanes and airships were used mainly for observation – just as they had been used in the land war. In the naval Battle of Jutland in 1916, German ships were first spotted by an observation plane.

Airships could stay airborne for many hours. Over the sea, it was difficult for the enemy to intercept them with airplanes or shoot at them with anti-aircraft guns. The airships just tried to stay out of trouble and report what they saw. Sometimes aircraft were used to attack.

On Patrol
Small British airships like this Sea Scout (SS) flew 60,000 hours of patrols around the British Isles, looking for U-boats. A normal flight, called a sortie, lasted about seven hours, but a flight of 12 or even 24 hours was not unusual. German U-boats were spotted by British airships and attacked by the navy 49 times. Often, just the presence of an airship made it difficult for a U-boat to attack British ships.

THE PIRATE

Pirate Zeppelin L23 flew a total of 101 missions. The Zeppelin was shot down in August 1917. It was destroyed and all its crew died.

In 1915, for the very first time, an aircraft managed to sink a ship with an underwater missile called a torpedo. In April 1917, a German Zeppelin L23 airship released a boat into the water, which hijacked a Norwegian ship. The ship was packed with timber bound for processing in England.

FELIXSTOWE F.2A FLYING BOAT

The British Felixstowe F.2A flying boat was based on the American Curtiss H.4 plane. These huge flying boats could land at sea, and flew long patrols along the German shores. Sometimes they fought battles with German seaplanes.

BLOODY APRIL 1917

VON RICHTHOFEN

Manfred von Richthofen was called the Red Baron because his aircraft was painted bright red. He shot down 80 aircraft, more than any other pilot during World War I.

In April 1917, Canadian forces launched a major attack against the Germans. The plan was to reduce Allied deaths on the ground by using aircraft to observe and photograph German trenches. Unfortunately, British planes were shot down in large numbers. April 1917 became known as Bloody April.

Royal Flying Corps (RFC) pilots flew aircraft that were good for observation, but very easy to shoot down. Pilots were often sent straight out of flying school and into battle. British pilots could only expect to survive a few weeks at the front. RFC pilots outnumbered the German fighter pilots, but the Germans were more experienced.

Observation Balloons

Observation balloons were used by armies in trenches along the front lines of the war. They were used to co-ordinate troops on the ground and were a favorite target of aircraft. Unfortunately for enemy aircraft, balloons were protected by machine-guns and anti-aircraft cannons.

Many German pilots had flown observation planes before switching to single-seat fighters, so they knew how to attack allied aircraft. The most famous German pilot was Manfred von Richthofen, the Red Baron, who shot down 21 aircraft in April 1917. His formation of brightly-colored planes was nicknamed The Flying Circus.

SHOT DOWN IN FLAMES

Most pilots feared fire more than anything else. They did not wear parachutes but some preferred to jump rather than burn up on the way down.

THE PREY

The F.E.2 plane was an outdated observation plane that was a favorite target of German fighters during Bloody April. A total of 58 F.E.2 planes were shot down. Only the B.E.2 (which was even more old fashioned) suffered heavier casualties.

ACES

Pilots and their crew did dangerous jobs during World War I. The best fighter pilots became heroes, and legends of their time. Some survived the war and some did not.

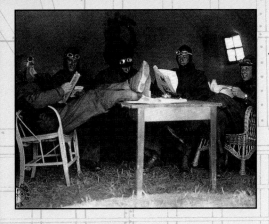

RECREATION

Pilots entertained themselves by playing games during the long, nervous hours on the ground.

J.T.B. McCUDDEN

Nationality: British
Victories: 57
Born: March 28, 1895
Died: July 9, 1918 (Flying accident)
A natural leader – he based his flying style on a careful study of fighter tactics.

EDWARD 'MICK' MANNOCK

Nationality: British
Victories: 73
Born: May 24, 1887
Died: July 26, 1918 (Killed in action)
Britain's highest scoring ace. He crashed in flames when his S.E.5 was hit by a stray bullet.

W.A. 'BILLY' BISHOP

Nationality: Canadian
Victories: 72
Born: February 8, 1894
Died: September 11, 1956
Canada's highest scoring ace of the war.

CHARLES NUNGESSER

Nationality: French
Victories: 43
Born: March 15, 1892
Died: May 8, 1927 (Lost at sea)
Nungesser was a French adventurer who became a famous ace, despite being shot down several times. In 1927, he disappeared during a flight over the Atlantic.

GEORGES GUYNEMER

Nationality: French
Victories: 53
Born: December 24, 1894
Died: September 11, 1917 (Killed in action)
Guynemer was a very aggressive fighter pilot who became a popular hero in the French press.

EDDIE RICKENBACKER

Nationality: American
Victories: 26
Born: October 8, 1890
Died: July 27, 1973
The top scoring American ace. After the war he helped to establish Eastern Airlines.

FIGHTERS

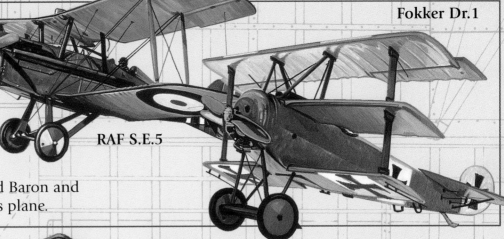

Fokker Dr.1

These two fighters are always associated with the aces. The British S.E.5 was flown by pilots such as McCudden and Mannock. The German Fokker Dr.1 triplane was not in widespread use, but it has become one of the best known fighters ever, because both the Red Baron and Werner Voss were killed flying this plane.

RAF S.E.5

ERNST UDET

Nationality: German
Victories: 62
Born: April 26, 1896
Died: November 17, 1941
A parachute saved the life of this German ace on two occasions. Very few aviators had a parachute. Udet's parachute was a gift from his father.

Marjorie Stinson
Women did not fly in combat in World War I. Marjorie Stinson and her sister, who were both pilots, established a flying school in Texas, with help from their mother. Their school trained hundreds of aviators to fly during the war.

WERNER VOSS

Nationality: German
Victories: 48
Born: 13 April, 1897
Died: 23 September, 1917 (Killed in action)
An expert pilot, he was killed in a Fokker Dr.1, in combat with seven S.E.5s.

DECORATIONS

Aces were awarded medals by their countries, especially in France and Germany. Newspapers compared them to heroic medieval knights, although fighter pilots only survived if they attacked from behind. This was a simple recipe for survival.

UNITED STATES
Medal of Honor

GERMANY
Iron Cross

FRANCE
Légion d'Honneur

BRITAIN
Victoria Cross

TRIAL AND ERROR

Good pilots needed good aircraft to survive in combat. The British ace Lanoe Hawker was said to be a better pilot than the Red Baron, but Hawker was killed by the Red Baron after a long fight, because the Baron flew a better plane.

ANTHONY H.G. FOKKER
Anthony Fokker was Dutch, but he built combat aircraft for the Germans during World War I. He offered to design planes for the Allies but unfortunately, his offer was turned down.

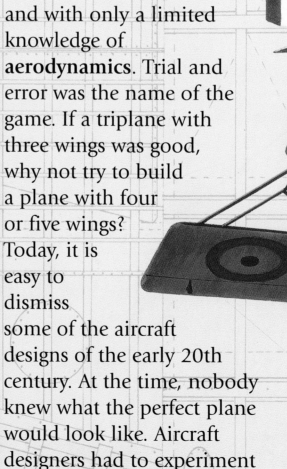

Aircraft designers tried hard to keep ahead of the enemy. New types of plane were designed, built, and tested in a matter of weeks. Today, it takes several years, or even decades, to design a military aircraft. Designing was done without the aid of computers and with only a limited knowledge of **aerodynamics**. Trial and error was the name of the game. If a triplane with three wings was good, why not try to build a plane with four or five wings? Today, it is easy to dismiss some of the aircraft designs of the early 20th century. At the time, nobody knew what the perfect plane would look like. Aircraft designers had to experiment with different designs.

Aircraft Factories

Thousand of airplanes were built in factories during the war. The planes were usually wooden frames that were put together by carpenters. The open wooden frames were braced with metal wires and covered with fabric. The fabric was made airtight with a lacquer called dope. If they were well built, these airplanes were light and very strong, too.

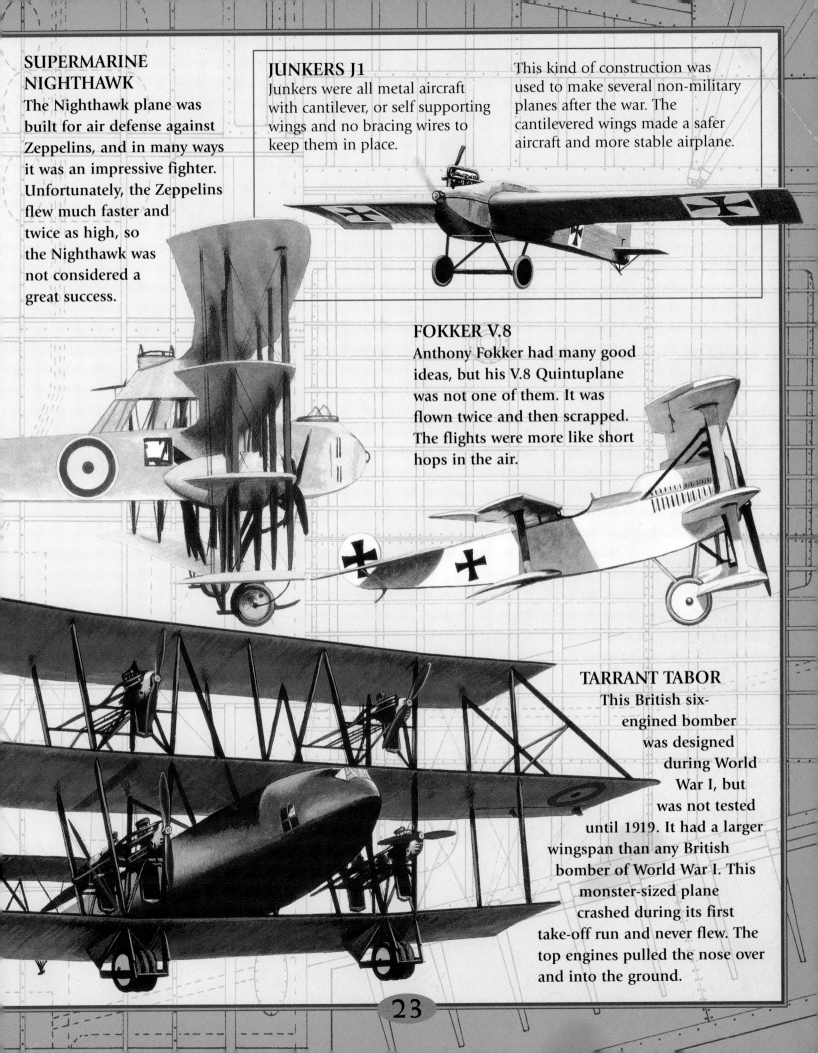

SUPERMARINE NIGHTHAWK

The Nighthawk plane was built for air defense against Zeppelins, and in many ways it was an impressive fighter. Unfortunately, the Zeppelins flew much faster and twice as high, so the Nighthawk was not considered a great success.

JUNKERS J1

Junkers were all metal aircraft with cantilever, or self supporting wings and no bracing wires to keep them in place.

This kind of construction was used to make several non-military planes after the war. The cantilevered wings made a safer aircraft and more stable airplane.

FOKKER V.8

Anthony Fokker had many good ideas, but his V.8 Quintuplane was not one of them. It was flown twice and then scrapped. The flights were more like short hops in the air.

TARRANT TABOR

This British six-engined bomber was designed during World War I, but was not tested until 1919. It had a larger wingspan than any British bomber of World War I. This monster-sized plane crashed during its first take-off run and never flew. The top engines pulled the nose over and into the ground.

23

HANGAR ATTACK
Each attacking Camel carried three small bombs, enough to set the hydrogen-filled Zeppelins ablaze. At Tondern, Germany, flames rose 984 feet (300 m) above the hangar. The Germans had not imagined that British aircraft could attack so far from home. They failed to shoot down any of the Camels.

SOPWITH CAMEL
The Sopwith Camel was easy to **maneuver**, could turn extremely fast, and was a deadly aircraft in the hands of a good pilot. It was also very difficult to fly and many pilots died in accidents trying to learn how to master the Camel.

AIRCRAFT CARRIERS

Airplanes had already been flown from ships before World War I, but it was only during the war that the first aircraft carriers were made. Fighter planes only carried enough fuel to carry them a small distance, so Britain needed ships to transport these planes and stop the Zeppelins over the sea.

Carrier-based aircraft attacked a land target for the first time in July 1918. They raided the Zeppelin base at Tondern, Germany and destroyed two Zeppelins stored in a large hangar. Shocked German troops came running out, firing rifles at the aircraft, but the British Sopwith Camel attack planes dove to about 50 feet (15 m) and zigzagged away over the flat marshy fields. Three Camel planes ran out of fuel and landed on the west coast of Denmark, which was a **neutral country**.

AIRCRAFT ON BOARD

For the Tondern attack, the seven British Camel airplanes took off from the converted deck of the HMS Furious cruiser. They were unable to land again on the flight deck. The pilots had to ditch in 10-foot (3-m) waves and wait to be picked up by a destroyer.

Eugene Ely

In 1910, American pilot Eugene Ely flew a Curtiss biplane from a platform built on a U.S. warship. This was the first time an aircraft had taken off from a ship. Two months later, in 1911, Ely became the first person to land on a ship. His aircraft was stopped by an arrester hook, which caught wires laid across the deck. This system is still used on aircraft carriers.

GROUND ATTACK

DANGEROUS WORK
Attacking trenches at low level with slow biplanes was very dangerous – and British pilots still did not wear parachutes. Half of the pilots sent out on these missions were killed during the last months of the war.

During the war, Zeppelins and other aircraft bombed factories and cities behind the front. They did damage but it made no difference to the outcome of the war. In 1918, ground attack aircraft changed how war was fought.

During the long years of **trench warfare**, it was difficult to break through the enemy lines of defense. Millions of soldiers died trying, but the battle lines hardly moved at all.

In 1918, large numbers of American troops joined the battle on the Western Front. The British army started to let **infantry**, tanks, and ground attack aircraft work together. This was a very good move, because the Germans found it difficult to defend themselves against all these different threats at the same time. German soldiers retreated toward Germany. They were losing the war.

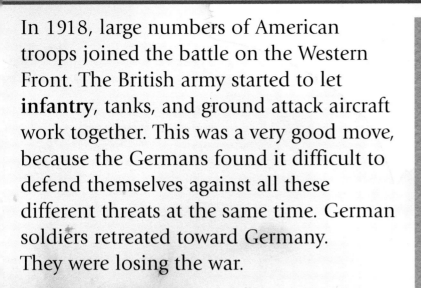

Escadrille Lafayette
American volunteers had been flying with the French Air Force since 1916. In 1918, when American troops joined the war in large numbers, the Escadrille Lafayette became the first American fighter squadron. Escadrille Lafayette's high-scoring pilots became commanders of other American squadrons.

COMBINED ATTACK
Sopwith Camels often took part in the combined attacks with ground troops and tanks. Camel pilots helped win the war, but paid a high price. In September 1918, more Camels were lost than any other type of Allied aircraft.

BOMBER
In 1918, the huge Handley Page 0/400 bombers were used to hit targets such as rail yards behind the German front. They also attacked cities in Western Germany. The 0/400 had the same wingspan as the Lancaster bomber of World War II, but the total take-off weight of the 0/400 was less than the weight of a Lancaster's bomb load.

THE LAST BATTLE

GEORGE BARKER

George Barker chose to volunteer for the Flying Corps, rather than fight in the mud of the trenches. He was a good pilot, and shot down 52 enemy aircraft. He died in a crash in 1930, 12 years after the war ended.

Soldiers and airmen fought and died right up until the very end of the war. Canadian ace pilot William George Barker fought many German Fokker D.VII planes a few weeks before the war ended.

Barker was one of the few pilots who survived years of combat flying. On October 27, 1918, he took off in his Sopwith Snipe plane from an airfield in France, to return to Britain. He soon spotted a German two-seater and shot it down. The attack was a mistake, and Barker fell into a trap. Soon the latest German Fokker D.VII fighters were swarming all around him. He fought desperately and claimed to have shot down four of the Germans before crash landing.

Still Flying

Aircraft from World War I can still be seen in museums around the world. Some are replicas, while others are genuine aircraft from the first war in the air. A few, such as this Sopwith triplane, are still flying. You might be lucky enough to see one at an airshow.

Barker was badly wounded, but survived thanks to his expert flying, although he never bragged about the fight. Barker was in the hospital when the war ended, at the eleventh hour of the eleventh day of the eleventh month of 1918. He was unable to sit up for three months.

STAYING WARM

As World War I went on, airmen flew higher and higher. George Barker got into his famous fight 21,000 feet (6,000 m) up, where it is about 89°F (35°C) colder than on the ground. Flying high meant discomfort in the cold, open cockpits. Pilots dressed in layers of clothing but still had trouble keeping warm. The lack of **oxygen** in the air at high level was another problem they faced.

RUMOURS

Newspapers of the day wrote that Barker fought against 60 Fokkers, although it was probably far fewer.

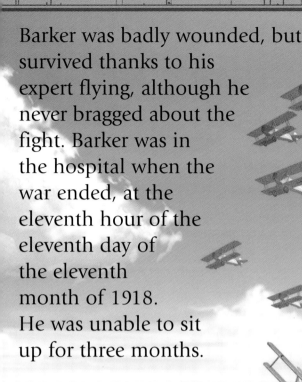

SPOTTERS' GUIDE

Military aircraft developed dramatically during World War I. In just four years, airplanes changed from being slow and difficult to maneuver to being fast and agile. Aircraft at the end of the war had twice the power of early war planes.

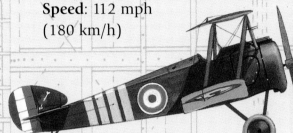

SIEMENS SCHUCKERT D III
Country: Germany
Description: Single-seat fighter
Length: 18 ft 8 in (6.7 m)
Wingspan: 27 ft 8 in (8.4 m)
Speed: 112 mph (180 km/h)

FOKKER DR.1
Country: Germany
Description: Single-seat fighter
Length: 19 ft 11 in (5.8 m)
Wingspan: 23 ft 7 in (7.2 m)
Speed: 115 mph (185 km/h)

GOTHA G V
Country: Germany
Description: Bomber
Length: 38 ft 11 in (11.9 m)
Wingspan: 77 ft 9 in (23.7 m)
Speed: 87 mph (140 km/h)

SOPWITH CAMEL
Country: Great Britain
Description: Single-seat fighter
Length: 18 ft 9 in (5.7 m)
Wingspan: 28 ft (8.5 m)
Speed: 115 mph (185 km/h)

SPAD S.XIII
Country: France
Description: Single-seat fighter
Length: 20 ft 8 in (6.3 m)
Wingspan: 26 ft 7 in (8.1 m)
Speed: 139 mph (224 km/h)

ROYAL AIRCRAFT FACTORY S.E.5A
Country: Great Britain
Description: Single-seater fighter/spotter
Length: 20 ft 11 in (6.4 m)
Wingspan: 26 ft 7 in (8.1 m)
Speed: 138 mph (222 km/h)

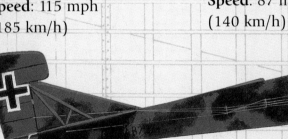

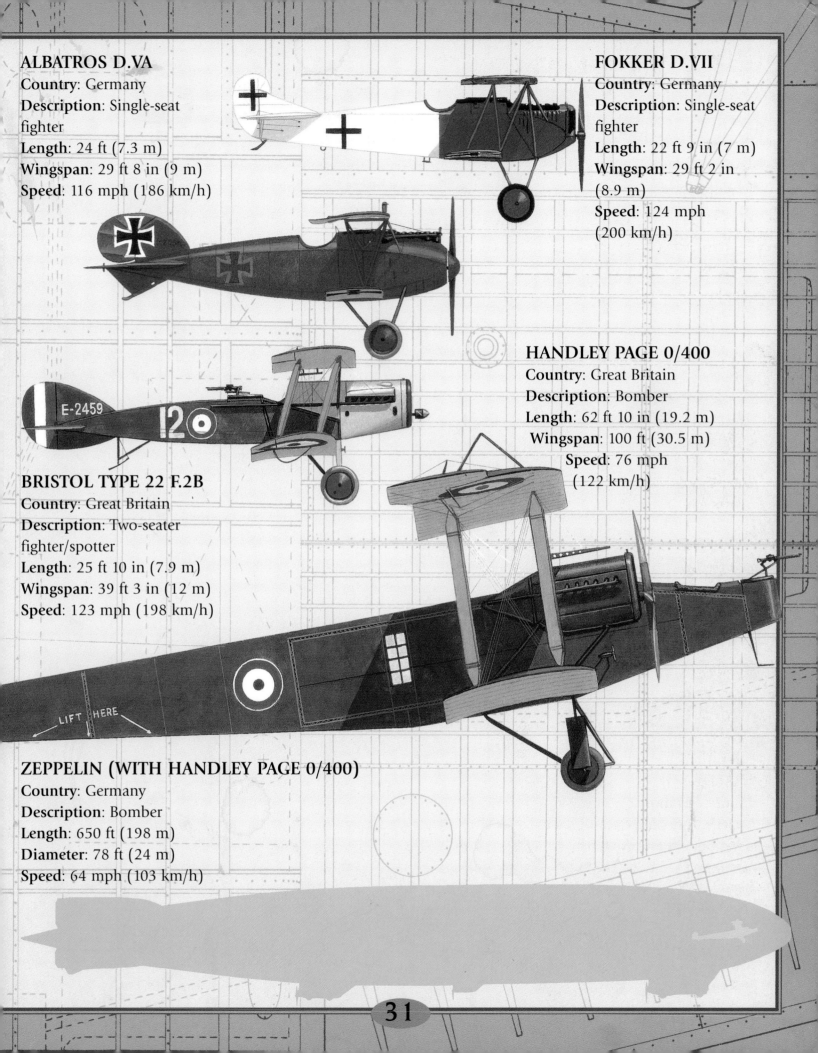

ALBATROS D.VA
Country: Germany
Description: Single-seat fighter
Length: 24 ft (7.3 m)
Wingspan: 29 ft 8 in (9 m)
Speed: 116 mph (186 km/h)

FOKKER D.VII
Country: Germany
Description: Single-seat fighter
Length: 22 ft 9 in (7 m)
Wingspan: 29 ft 2 in (8.9 m)
Speed: 124 mph (200 km/h)

HANDLEY PAGE 0/400
Country: Great Britain
Description: Bomber
Length: 62 ft 10 in (19.2 m)
Wingspan: 100 ft (30.5 m)
Speed: 76 mph (122 km/h)

BRISTOL TYPE 22 F.2B
Country: Great Britain
Description: Two-seater fighter/spotter
Length: 25 ft 10 in (7.9 m)
Wingspan: 39 ft 3 in (12 m)
Speed: 123 mph (198 km/h)

ZEPPELIN (WITH HANDLEY PAGE 0/400)
Country: Germany
Description: Bomber
Length: 650 ft (198 m)
Diameter: 78 ft (24 m)
Speed: 64 mph (103 km/h)

INDEX

GLOSSARY

AERODYNAMICS An airplane or vehicle with round edges and smooth surfaces that reduce wind drag and allow the plane to go faster.

AIRSHIP A self-propelled aircraft filled with a lighter than air gas.

ALLIES The nations that joined to fight against the Central Powers in World War I, including the British Empire, France, the Russian Empire, and the United States.

ARTILLERY Large heavy guns and the group of people, or part of the army who operate them.

DESTROYER A small but fast warship armed with guns and torpedos.

DICTA Firmly-stated rules.

EASTERN FRONT The war front that ran along the Russian border from the Baltic Sea to the Black Sea.

FRONT LINES The most forward line or group of combat in war.

GONDOLA A basket or cabin of an airship.

INFANTRY Army units that were trained to fight on foot.

INTERNATIONAL CONVENTION A meeting of representatives from countries all over the world to discuss an issue and make decisions.

MANEUVER To control or change the movement of a vehicle.

MUNITIONS Guns, ammunition, and other supplies used for warfare.

NEUTRAL COUNTRY A country that is not aligned with or supporting a side during a war.

OXYGEN The air we breathe.

TRENCH WARFARE War fought in trenches dug into the ground. World War I was the first major conflict to involve trenches.

VICTORIA CROSS A medal awarded to soldiers of the British Empire for acts of bravery.

WESTERN FRONT The war front that ran through Belgium to France and Switzerland.